# How to Get the Most Out of Attending a Conference

By Shawn Collins

**Copyright © by Affiliate Summit 2013**

All Rights Reserved. No part of this publication may be reproduced in any form or by any means, including scanning, photocopying, or otherwise without prior written permission of the copyright holder.

# Table of Contents

**INTRODUCTION** .................................................................. 5
**BEFORE THE CONFERENCE** ............................................ 9
   Define Goals and Measurable Objectives ............................ 10
   Get a Wingman/Woman for Networking ................................ 11
   Read Your Confirmation Email ............................................. 12
   Subscribe to the Conference Newsletter ............................. 13
   Participate in Conference Social Network ........................... 14
   Follow the Twitter Hashtag and Conference Twitter Account ... 15
   Plan to Wake Early, Stay Late .............................................. 16
   Never Eat Alone .................................................................... 17
   Install the Conference App ................................................... 19
   Work Out Your Schedule ...................................................... 20
   Stay in the Conference Hotel ............................................... 22
   Prepare Follow-Up Materials ................................................ 24
   Don't Leave Your Travel Up in the Air .................................. 25
   Networking for Introverts ...................................................... 26
**DURING THE CONFERENCE** ........................................... 29
   Check-in Early ....................................................................... 30
   Map Out the Conference ...................................................... 31
   Conference Time is Networking Time .................................. 32
   Keys to an Effective Networking Conversation ................... 33
   When to Look at Conference Badges .................................. 35
   Have a System for Business Cards ..................................... 36
   The Benefits of Attending Sessions ..................................... 37
   Say What You Like and Dislike ............................................. 38
   Competitive Intelligence ........................................................ 39

Don't Rely on the Wi-Fi ..................................................................40
Charge Your Devices Each Night ...............................................41
Don't Waste Time on Random Booths ......................................42
Stay Hydrated .................................................................................43
Leave Space in Your Luggage ....................................................44
Get Off Your Computer .................................................................45
Follow Up Immediately .................................................................46
Don't Lose Control ........................................................................47
**AFTER THE CONFERENCE** ..................................................**48**
Follow Up After the Conference .................................................49
**BONUS: PACKING CHECKLIST** ...............................................**51**
**About Affiliate Summit** ..............................................................**54**

# INTRODUCTION

Do you remember how you felt on the first day at a new school? If you were like me, it was equal parts anxiety, dread, and disorientation. Lots of people milling around, and they all seemed to know each other, but I didn't know any of them.

It was similar the first time I went to a conference. I was rushed through the check-in line, given my badge and attendee bag, and just pushed on to figure things out. I didn't know who was who - it was a blur of nametags racing by me.

But where were they all going? I had no idea. I felt like I was a stranger in a strange land.

So I sat in a corner, put on some headphones, and dug into my bag of conference information. There was a schedule with lots of things going on at the same time, and I didn't know where to begin. My eyes glazed over, and I felt sort of helpless.

When it came time for lunch, I left the hotel and grabbed some food at a local restaurant by myself. I don't think I really talked to anybody at the whole conference.

One big problem was that I went into the whole thing without a plan. I just showed up and expected I'd just magically get it. My lack of advance planning made the time spent there, as well as the money for the trip, into a big waste.

When I got back to the office, I told the boss how lame it was, and how I wouldn't recommend returning next year.

The next time I was sent to a conference, I made sure to do some homework in advance to figure out who I might want to meet, as well as educational sessions that might benefit me. It was a far more worthwhile use of my time.

I came to realize that going to a conference is an investment, rather than an expense. It's not just an investment of money, but time, too. But when you do take the time to maximize the opportunities, the experience can be fulfilling and prosperous.

After I understood that there were two reasons for me to attend these sorts of events, networking and education, I became better and better at planning and organizing my time.

The whole process of attending a conference isn't limited to the time you are physically there with a badge around your neck. In order to make the most of it, there are things you can and should be doing before, during, and after the conference.

Over the years, I've worked up lots of strategies, and learned things from other folks to get the maximum value from attending conferences.

When Missy Ward and I started up the Affiliate Summit conference in 2003, we crafted it based on our frustrations and experiences as conference attendees, and we've evolved things over the years to make it the best environment we can for the people who attend.

However, it's still up to the individual attendee to seize opportunities and get the most out of the experience.

In the following pages, I share a whole bunch of things I would suggest you do when you sign up to attend future conferences. I am using conference here as an overall term to cover conventions, tradeshows, seminars, and any other sort of meetings where you can learn and network.

It isn't necessary to read this book from front to back - you can jump around and pull out the tips and ideas that interest you. But please don't just read this book. Take action, too!

# BEFORE THE CONFERENCE

## Define Goals and Measurable Objectives

Before you even register for a conference, it's essential that you have a sense for what you're planning to accomplish by attending.

Are you trying to make a statement by your attendance, or do you simply hope to work out some deals and learn the latest and greatest?

Some people go to a conference to spread the word about a new product or service, or just to get the brand out there. Others want to network like crazy and/or act as a sponge in educational sessions, so they can learn best practices, tips, industry changes, etc.

But then there are people who turn up at a conference with no game plan. Don't do that. You're better off staying home.

Whatever the reason that you decide to attend, you should work out your goals and objectives at the time you register for the conference, and then begin working on how you will accomplish them.

## Get a Wingman/Woman for Networking

Do you know anybody else who is going to the next conference you're attending? If not, start asking around in social media and industry forums.

It's easier to meet people when you're going around a conference with somebody.

Also, it's helpful to have that person to compare notes on things, especially if you split up to catch different sessions that you both wanted to attend.

## Read Your Confirmation Email

You ought to receive a confirmation email shortly after registering for the conference. Be sure to read it, so you don't miss any important information.

Also, whitelist the sending address and keep that email.

Check whether it has your registration information in it, and be sure there are no typos, because that's what they're going to use for your badge. If you made a typo, reach out to the conference organizers to update your information, so you don't have to deal with it at the conference.

If you don't receive the email confirmation within an hour or so, contact the conference to inquire about your registration. Maybe there was a problem processing your payment or some other issue.

## Subscribe to the Conference Newsletter

There are lots of opportunities, events, tools, deadlines, and tricks shared by conference organizers in their email newsletters, and I would highly recommend subscribing.

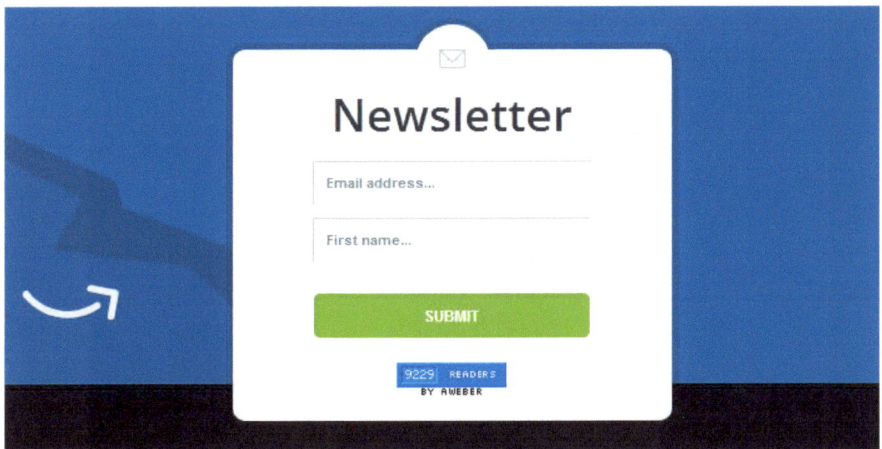

I can't tell you how many times I've heard attendees say, "I wish I knew about this before the conference…"

Additionally, keep an eye on their Facebook, Twitter, and YouTube accounts for information related to the upcoming conference.

In the case of the Affiliate Summit conference, we post all of our news to our blog, and then it's summarized weekly in our newsletter.

That information also goes out to Facebook and Twitter, so attendees can consume it in the place they prefer.

## Participate in Conference Social Network

Most conferences will have some sort of network or group setup for the purpose of bringing together conference attendees for advance networking.

Some might have software dedicated to networking, while others create a private group on Facebook or somewhere else.

After you've joined, fill out your profile, so people are able to determine if you are somebody that makes sense meeting. If there is no profile in your particular social network, post an introduction that provides a brief bio and what you're trying to accomplish at the conference.

That will make it easier for relevant attendees to come to you. Also, seek out others who you hope to meet and make that initial connection.

## Follow the Twitter Hashtag and Conference Twitter Account

Many conferences will share a hashtag in advance, so that attendees can stay on top of what's going on during the conference.

A hashtag is a keyword preceded by the pound sign (#), and it is included when people post a Tweet related to the conference, such as an impromptu happy hour or a really good session.

For instance, the hashtag for the Affiliate Summit West 2014 conference was set as #ASW14, and searching Twitter for that hashtag before, during, and after the conference would result in Tweets related to the conference.

Also, a lot of conferences have a dedicated Twitter account, where they make official announcements, share last minute changes to the agenda, etc.

Be sure to check whether any conference you attend has a Twitter account, so you can follow it and stay on top of things.

## Plan to Wake Early, Stay Late

I wouldn't typically advise you to skimp on sleep and run yourself ragged, but it's tough to avoid it at a conference.

You're in a city with a large bunch of industry folks, way more than you can talk to while you're there, so it can be worth it to sacrifice time in the fluffy hotel bed. Don't sleep away opportunities.

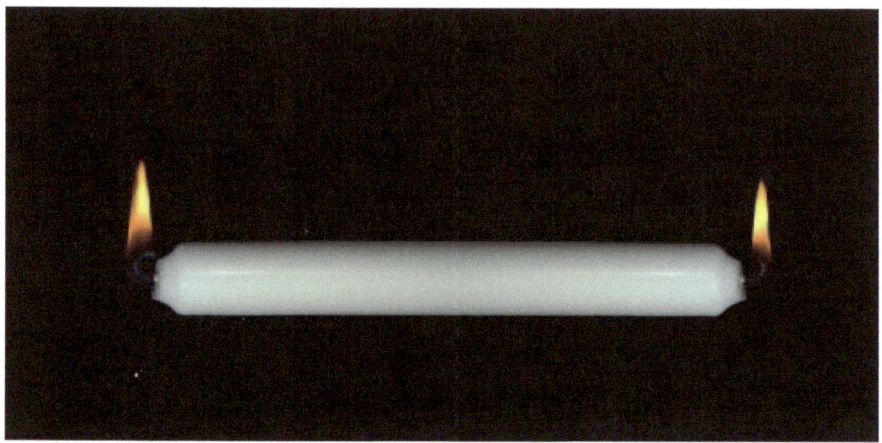

Also, a lot of the best relationship building takes place in the informal settings after hours in the conference hotel bar(s) and lobby.

So, burn the candle at both ends for a few days. Get some sleep, stay hydrated, and don't skip meals, but plan to take advantage of the temporary opportunities that are there for you.

## Never Eat Alone

One of my favorite business books is "Never Eat Alone: And Other Secrets to Success, One Relationship at a Time" by Keith Ferrazzi, and I would suggest reading it in the near future.

But for now, I am just touching on the title of his book.

Meals at a conference are a great time to meet multiple people and build on relationships. Be sure you have a pass that includes the conference meals, so you don't miss out on this precious networking time. If you don't have the right pass, inquire about an upgrade.

Then, at the conference, seek out tables of strangers and ask if it's OK to join them for meals. Get the introductions going and find out what everybody is doing and who they are.

And then try to identify whether you can help your new friends through something you do in your business or an introduction to somebody else at the conference.

If you can't get a pass that has access to the conference meals, try to organize a group to get together in a nearby restaurant.

The important thing is that you don't waste these meals by sleeping in or sneaking off to your room to catch up on email.

If you're not present for meals, you may just as well not be present for the conference.

## Install the Conference App

Find out if the conference has an app, and if they do, be sure in install it on your phone and/or tablet in advance of the conference.

A typical conference app will include the agenda, scheduling tools, networking functionality, speaker bios, and details on the sponsoring and exhibiting companies.

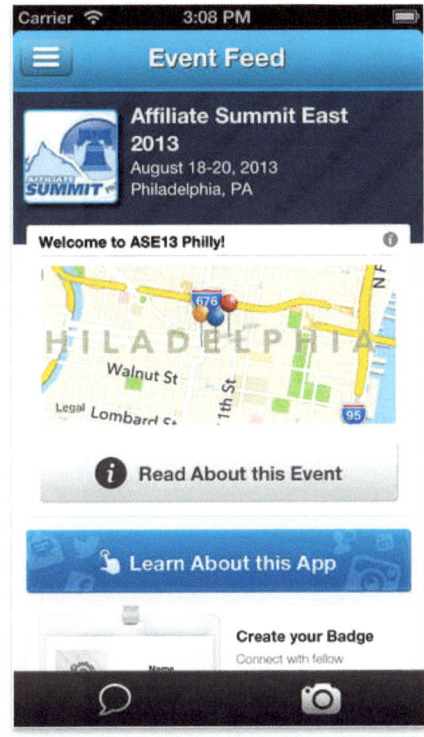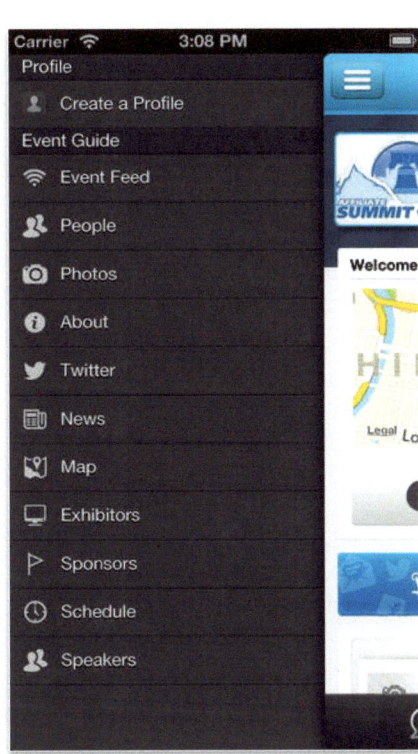

This can be invaluable during a conference, so you don't have to keep a copy of the physical program. Also, if there is a capability for networking, you should set up whatever you can in advance, so you can get optimal use of the app at the conference.

## Work Out Your Schedule

When the agenda is finalized online for the conference, you can start figuring out your schedule, so you know when you'll be occupied and which times are available for meetings.

Read through all of the session titles and descriptions, as well as the speakers for each, and pick your favorites. When I do this, it's a mix of the topics and people I want to see.

Start setting up meetings in advance in 15-30 minute slots as soon as you can, because the schedules of your fellow organized people tend to fill up fast.

Reach out to your contacts to let them know you will be at the conference, and that you are available to meet.

Mention that you'll be there on your Facebook, Google+, LinkedIn, and Twitter accounts, so people know you're there, and you might be able to setup times with folks you've wanted to meet and didn't realize they'd be attending, too.

Also, you can certainly drop in randomly at the exhibit hall booths of companies you want to meet, but you're more likely to get time with the right person if you book a specific time before the conference.

## Stay in the Conference Hotel

Conferences will often have a group rate at a hotel for attendees, whether the event is taking place in the hotel or a local convention center.

There are a number of benefits to booking in the conference hotel, and it's important to book as early as you can, so you don't risk the spots filling up.

You can't beat the convenience when the sleeping rooms are in the same building as the conference. It's always nice to have your things an elevator away if you forget something.

Also, big concentrations of conference attendees stay at the hotel, so they tend to hang out there after hours, as well as for coffee in the morning.

This is when so much of the quality networking happens, because you have a good chance to make serendipitous connections in the lobby, bar, restaurant, elevator, etc.

Wherever you decide to say, print out your hotel name, address, and confirmation, so you know where to go when you land (some cities have many hotels from the same chain in different locations), and you can limit issues at check-in.

**Prepare Follow-Up Materials**

You'll want to follow up soon after the conference with your new connections.

Whether it's sending a note or some literature, brochures, sales kits, etc., you should get all of these materials together before you leave.

That way you can knock out your follow ups shortly after returning home from the conference.

## Don't Leave Your Travel Up in the Air

It takes some homework to get the best rates for a flight, but there are some things to bear in mind, so you don't pay more than you have to.

Airline prices typically increase with two weeks to go before a flight, so it's a good idea to secure your flight when you register for the conference.

Sometimes you can get a great price at the last minute, but don't count on getting lucky.

How will you get to and from the airport in the conference city? Is there a hotel shuttle? Trains? Maybe cabs are the easiest way to go. Work it out in advance and the trip from the airport to and from the hotel can be stress free.

Finally, check the latest TSA and airline guidelines, so you can avoid headaches at the airport.

## Networking for Introverts

Hello, my name is Shawn and I'm an introvert.

I've been going to conferences for about 15 years. I was aware right away that they weren't the sort of environment I preferred, since a main objective is to constantly strike up conversations with strangers to network.

That just wasn't in my nature. I was used to lots of labels for me, like shy, quiet, reserved. Then I came across a whole new label that never occurred to me before... introvert.

Somebody on Facebook mentioned the book, "Quiet: The Power of Introverts in a World That Can't Stop Talking" by Susan Cain, and I was curious, so I ordered it.

I was fascinated at how spot on the description of an introvert fit me. Cain defines introverts as those who prefer less stimulating environments and tend to enjoy quiet concentration, listen more than they talk, and think before they speak.

And I know I'm not alone with this at conferences, as Cain states that one third to half of Americans are believed to be introverts.

So, here are some strategies I've employed over the years to make networking easier for me.

1. **Pre-network**. There are lots of opportunities to reach out to fellow attendees in advance of a conference, such as a group on Facebook created for attendees, following the hashtag on Twitter, using the app for the event, and reaching out to speakers (they're on the site months before the conference).

2. **Be prepared**. Set up meetings in advance. Practice your elevator speech. Have questions ready to ask when chatting with new people, and be a good listener.

3. **Start with a smile**. You don't have to be the one that breaks the ice, but you should be approachable. Burying your face in your phone or standing in the corner with your arms folded will guarantee a barrier around you. Just smile. People will walk up and start talking.

4. **Get a conference friend**. With your pre-networking, go and find somebody to be your wingman – it makes it way easier to meet people. We created a program for first time attendees of Affiliate Summit, called the Newcomers Program, where attendees can get matched up with conference veterans to help them navigate the conference. Do this if it's an option at your next conference!

5. **Just be there**. It can be tempting to decide you're backed up on work and then camp out in your hotel room. Don't do that. Be with people as much as possible. Take some breaks away to recharge, but not too many.

6. **Become a speaker**. I don't like speaking, either. I still get nervous. But it's great exposure, plus it results in people seeking you out.

Come on out and network in your way, introverts. Try these strategies to make your next conference the most productive time it can be for you.

# DURING THE CONFERENCE

## Check-in Early

Pick up conference materials as early as possible - check the agenda to find out when is the earliest that you can get your badge, attendee bad, and any other items.

Otherwise, you will risk spending a lot of time in lines. That's precious time that is wasted unnecessarily.

Also, this is a great time to ask any questions you have, because the staff is not swamped, yet.

## Map Out the Conference

Get the show map and cruise the conference area to know where things are and be ready to go on the first morning.

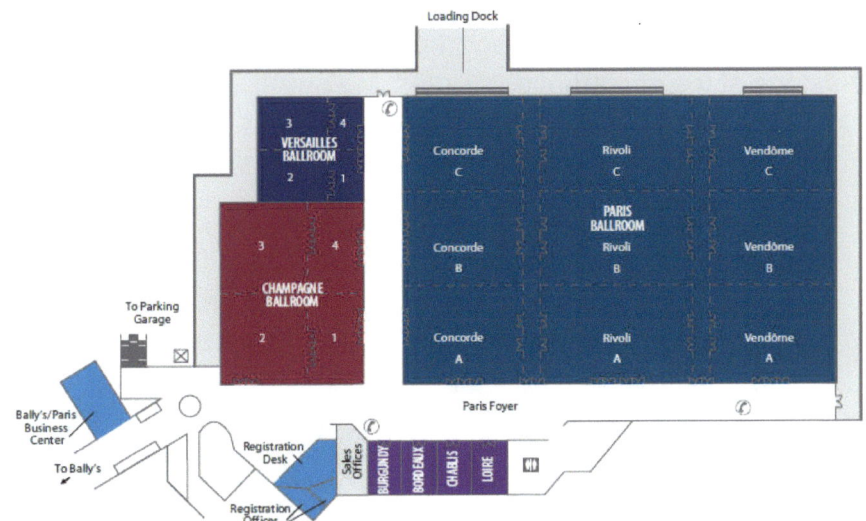

Go through the agenda, so you can figure out where to go for cocktail parties, roundtable discussions, meals, coffee breaks, etc.

Do a dry run and get oriented with the locations of the rooms in relation to the elevators, lobby, your room, etc.

I can't tell you how many times I've heard from people who were complaining about being perpetually lost at a conference hotel. Don't waste your time like them.

## Conference Time is Networking Time

Even if you're going to a conference with the primary goal of learning new things, you will also be networking. It's inevitable.

Just so we're clear, networking should be about relationship building for you. It's really any interaction you have with fellow attendees at the conference.

It's to your benefit to meet as many people as you can in your industry and build relationships. But don't make it a numbers game.

Nobody gets a prize for collecting the most business cards. The prize is in the relationships, so take the time to get to know people and find out what they do and what they need.

Some folks might be just right for you to work with, and others might not have a clear benefit to you. So, think about how you might benefit them. They just might be the connection that brings you your next great relationship.

## Keys to an Effective Networking Conversation

The conversation you have at a conference a typically brief, so it's key to be clear and concise about what you can do for other people and what you need.

Instead of going right in with a pitch, ask questions about them and what they want and need. Nobody wants to hear your pitch, but people love to talk about themselves and what they're trying to get out of being there.

Be sure to keep it brief. Think of the K.I.S.S. method (Keep It Simple, Stupid), because everybody is trying to meet lots of people. Make your chat a surgical strike, and leave details for later.

Basically, think of each encounter as an elevator pitch, not in that you are doing a hard sell, but for the time you have. Be brief about yourself, and try to keep them wanting to know more.

Since your opening lines are essentially the headline for your conversation, split test them. No, I am not kidding. Try different approaches and pay attention to what is most effective.

## When to Look at Conference Badges

You should be meeting new people at each conference, instead of staying in your comfort zone with people you already know, because new people = new business.

But the problem with new people is that you don't know their names, and it is awkward to have to gaze down at their badge. So, make it a point to peek at the badge before you approach them, and then your conversation will start more naturally.

Be social with the person eating next to you, people in hallways, next to you in sessions, during registration, and in the elevator. And always make it a habit to learn their name before you open your mouth (and while they're not looking).

While my schedule is packed at a given conference, I always schedule open time, so I can say hi to strangers and make new connections.

## Have a System for Business Cards

I keep my own business cards in my right pocket, and as I hand them to people I ask for their business card.

Also, I always have a pen on me to write notes on their card to remind me why I want to follow-up with them.

Then their business cards go in my left pocket.

I see some people use the name badge holder to store their cards or those that they receive.

Whichever way you do it, just work out some system, so you're not fishing for your business cards when you need them.

## The Benefits of Attending Sessions

The chance to learn is an obvious reason to attend sessions, but also you get access to the speakers, who are industry leaders in their specialty.

In addition to having the opportunity to ask questions during the Q&A period, it is also a big plus to be able to introduce yourself to the speakers after the session and set some groundwork for a relationship with them.

If you don't have a question for them after the session, just take a moment to introduce yourself and request their business card to follow up later.

**Say What You Like and Dislike**

Be sure to provide session and conference feedback, so they can fix the broken stuff and accentuate the positive.

This goes for the topics, speakers, venue, staff, food, and really any element of the conference.

As a conference organizer, I LOVE receiving feedback. It has led to many of the changes and innovations we've made over the years.

## Competitive Intelligence

You're at a conference for your industry, or it has some relation, so it's likely that your competition is there, too.

Maybe they even have a booth in the exhibit hall.

If that's the case, take the opportunity to pick-up their collateral. It's a great way to stay current on what they are doing, and to help you come up with ideas for your business.

But don't be a creeper that hangs out on the outskirts to eavesdrop on their conversations. That's just tacky and embarrassing.

**Don't Rely on the Wi-Fi**

It is expected that a conference will provide Wi-Fi, but don't depend on it.

The problem is that the connections can get quickly maxed out when people are connecting with multiple devices.

●●●●○ AT&T  LTE          6:07 AM          ⬈ ✱ 100% ▰

**❮** Settings **Personal Hotspot**

Personal Hotspot                                    ⬤

Now Discoverable.

Other users can look for your shared network using Wi-Fi and Bluetooth under the name "Shawn Collins iPhone".

Wi-Fi Password             GoToASE14  ❯

The vendors that supply the Wi-Fi have caps on the number of connections, so have a contingency plan.

Personally, I like to make my phone into a Hotspot, and I don't even bother with the conference Wi-Fi, but that's because I am paranoid and don't like to use public Wi-Fi.

## Charge Your Devices Each Night

Battery life seems to evaporate faster at a conference than anywhere else, so be sure to plug in your phone to get a full charge before you go to sleep each night.

Bring along a backup power source and/or charger during the day, too.

If you're lucky, there will be a power station at the conference.

## Don't Waste Time on Random Booths

Don't waste time on booths that don't interest you - time is money and 5 minutes here and there results in lots of time and lost opportunities.

This won't be an issue if you planned out which companies to visit in advance, and you did that, right?

If not, it's not too late during the conference. Read through the company descriptions for the exhibitors and figure out which you want to visit.

## Stay Hydrated

Drink lots of water morning, noon, and night. When I get settled at a conference, one of my moves is to run out and buy water at a local Walgreens or similar store.

You can get a 12-pack for cheap, so you don't have to resort to the $5 bottle in your hotel room.

While you are there, grab some snacks and caffeine sources, in case you're running low on energy.

Also, with all of the talking, you might get dry lips. Grab some lip balm, so you don't have that gummy white stuff on your lips when you're trying to do business.

Oh yeah, and some breath mints and gum. I don't care who you are - if you have dragon breath, I am instantly looking for an exit strategy from our conversation.

## Leave Space in Your Luggage

One of the most important things to bring in your suitcase is space, so you can bring back literature, sales kits, etc. from exhibitors.

And then there are the various promotional items. I've got four kids, so if an exhibitor has a stuffed animal or other tchotchke, I need four to maintain harmony at home.

I suppose some people only wear their undergarments one time and then throw them out. If that's the case, the space will magically be created.

## Get Off Your Computer

Yes, I know that sometimes urgent matters come up, and they have to be taken care of during the conference.

Real work is OK, of course.

But social media nonsense is not. Simply put, don't waste time and opportunities. Never sit against the wall in the hallway at a conference to watch a Daily Show segment or comment on some dopey rant from your friend on Facebook.

If being on your computer at a conference is optional, then opt to shut it down, and go take advantage of the educational and networking opportunities.

## Follow Up Immediately

You can't follow up too soon.

If there is downtime on the exhibit hall floor, start organizing business cards and leads right there. Finish this up in the hotel room later on.

This way you can actually fill holes in your meeting schedule while you are still at the conference.

Sometimes that is not possible, so get the business cards organized and follow up that night with an email and/or LinkedIn connection, and then a phone call the next day.

When you get back to the office, break out a pen and some thank you cards for some hand-written notes. Trust me, they have a nice impact.

**Don't Lose Control**

Remember that you are representing your company - you are not auditioning for the Hangover, Part 4.

Late night networking is great and can be really beneficial. But there is a fine line between networking and being a belligerent idiot.

OK, it's not a fine like - it's very clear. Remember why you are at the conference and keep your goals and objectives in mind.

You're not a rock star when you can't get out of bed for a breakfast meeting. You're a jackass.

# AFTER THE CONFERENCE

## Follow Up After the Conference

You spent all of that time before and during the conference working out goals and objectives, and then achieving them, so don't quit before you get to the finish line.

You have not finished until you've followed up with the people you chatted with during the conference.

Resist the temptation to do an email blast. Why, because it's easy, impersonal, and that's what every other half-ass will do (the complete asses won't bother to follow up).

Instead, lead with a handwritten note. Get some of those little folding "thank you" cards and scratch out quick notes to your new contacts.

No novels - just a couple or three sentences to further your conversation and setup a phone call.

In some cases, you'll also want to send out literature, brochures, sales kits, etc. Hopefully, you pulled together all of that stuff before the conference, and now it's ready to go in the mail.

If you don't hear back from that initial contact in a week, drop them an email or ring their phone to jumpstart the relationship.

Good luck!

# BONUS: PACKING CHECKLIST

You should make a checklist of what to bring and what to pack for the conference. I'll help you out here with the checklist I use to quickly pack without forgetting any essentials.

While some of these things won't apply to you, maybe they'll help give ideas or help you remember to grab something you were about to forget.

- Address of your hotel. Ever gotten to a city and forgot where you were staying. I have – what a pain.

- Phone, camera, laptop, and chargers.
- Small power strip, because there is often a plug shortage at hotel room desks.
- Cable to transfer pictures to your computer.
- Phone – seems automatic, but I got halfway to the airport before I realized I didn't have it a couple years ago. Also, install the conference app!
- Elevator pitch: summarize you company or latest project in about 15 seconds.
- Plenty of business cards. I've never regretted having to bring a stack home, but have kicked myself for running out.
- Comfortable shoes. Lots of walking around during a conference. Lots of people focus on looking good, and their feet are killing them. I wear sneakers that feel good, and I last all day without thinking about my feet.
- Printed agenda, so you can work up your schedule of where you want to go and whom you want to meet.
- Gum and/or cough drops for all of the talking and nice breath maintenance.
- Lip balm, since those lips get dry from all the talking and dry air.
- Purell or other hand sanitizer, since there are lots of germs at a conference.

- Vitamins and various medicines – I like to bring some a small selection of remedies for colds, headaches, sour stomachs, etc. Great to have on hand if needed.
- Cash money for tips, cabs, and other random expenses.
- Copies of your important documents, ID, and credit cards, either on paper or scanned to a protected area of your HD. In the event you lose your wallet or purse, you will be able to have some record of your identity.
- Printed out confirmations for your conference registration, flight, hotel, party RSVPs, etc.
- Extra paper and pens. I like to do a daily brain dump of ideas and plans, and then organize the thoughts on the trip home.

When you are days away from leaving for the conference, make it a point to watch the weather forecast, so you can switch out clothing for something more temperature appropriate if need be.

# About Affiliate Summit

Affiliate Summit was founded by Missy Ward and Shawn Collins in 2003 for the purpose of providing educational sessions on the latest industry issues and fostering a productive networking environment for affiliate marketers.

Get details on the next Affiliate Summit event at
http://www.affiliatesummit.com

Follow Affiliate Summit…

Facebook -- http://www.facebook.com/AffiliateSummit
Flickr -- http://www.flickr.com/photos/affsum/
Google+ -- https://plus.google.com/+Affiliatesummitconference
LinkedIn -- http://www.linkedin.com/groups/Affiliate-Summit-3906754
Pinterest -- http://www.pinterest.com/affiliatesummit/
Twitter -- http://twitter.com/affiliatesummit
YouTube -- http://www.youtube.com/affiliatesummit

www.ingramcontent.com/pod-product-compliance
Lightning Source LLC
Chambersburg PA
CBHW040900180526
45159CB00001B/471